Translations from Bark Beetle

Also by Jody Gladding

Rooms and Their Airs
Stone Crop

Translations from Bark Beetle   POEMS   Jody Gladding

milkweed
editions

(800) 520-6455
milkweed.org

Published 2014 by Milkweed Editions
Cover design by Jeenee Lee
Cover photo by Jeenee Lee. Ward's Natural Science
Establishment, Inc. specimen box, Rochester, N.Y.
Interior photographs by Emma Norman
Author photo by Jake Brillhart

This project is supported in part by the Vermont Arts
Council and the National Endowment for the Arts.

18 19 20 21 22   5 4 3 2

First Edition

Milkweed Editions, an independent nonprofit pub-
lisher, gratefully acknowledges sustaining support
from the Bush Foundation; the Patrick and Aimee
Butler Foundation; the Driscoll Foundation; the
Jerome Foundation; the Lindquist & Vennum Foundation;
the McKnight Foundation; the National Endowment for
the Arts; the Target Foundation; and other gener-
ous contributions from foundations, corporations,
and individuals. Also, this activity is made possi-
ble by the voters of Minnesota through a Minnesota
State Arts Board Operating Support grant, thanks to
a legislative appropriation from the arts and cul-
tural heritage fund, and a grant from the Wells Fargo
Foundation Minnesota. For a full listing
of Milkweed Editions supporters, please visit
milkweed.org.

Library of Congress
Cataloging-in-Publication Data

Gladding, Jody, 1955-
[Poems. Selections]
Translations from Bark Beetle : poems / Jody
Gladding. -- First Edition.
     pages cm
Includes bibliographical references.
ISBN 978-1-57531-455-0 (alk. paper) --
ISBN 978-1-57531-891-6 (ebook)
I. Title.
PS3557.L2914A6 2014
811'.54--dc23

2013042290

CONTENTS

Translations from Bark Beetle

1

Toward

becoming
some kind
of other
I've been so
at home
here   the ocean close
then farther away
home a place
in France
a preposition
I've grown
from   apart
of speech

Spending Most of Their Time in Galleries, Adults Come into the Open on Warm Sunny Days: Translations from Bark Beetle

1

•'ve learned through wood
yo• can only travel in one direction
but turn again with m• there love
sap in the chamber
red the friable
taste of yo• •'ve learned
there are other ways in the wood's
growing
if not for m•--
find hollow
find spell

2

o•r animal shifts in the leaves its leg asleep
not fodder nothing for good
surely m•y neighbor knew
overhead this morning is just this love at work in •s
the difference between abundance
if roofs find time a burden the busy
emergent
yes--rescinded
white flake and more falling

1 - complete

2 - fragments

Translator's note: Certain elements of the grammar make translating Bark Beetle problematic. There are only two verb tenses: the cyclical and the radiant. Prepositional phrases figure prominently and seem necessary for a complete synctactical unit. The same pronoun form (indicated as •) is used for first and second person in singular, plural, and all cases.

Engraver Beetle Cycle

●   through work the quietly
puncture begins in a dark
if not there's no
         telling
(rue mores of light and lying)
some have remained here burrowed
m●y sweet m●y rolled
m●y x as in xylem
cambrial   phloem   corridor
● think ●'m repeating m●yself
there are rumors of flight and fungi
         (of light and lying)
the death of a tree's

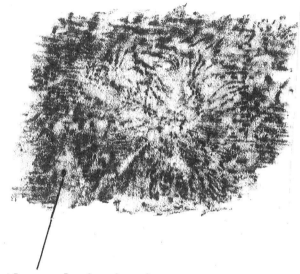

engraver beetle cycle begins here

Sonogram of Raven Calls

rapp

krapp

kra

pruk

quork

gro

kaah

kaa

krrk

nuk

kwulkulkkul

caw

caw

cawlup

awk

cluck

kow

ku-uk-kuk

ko-pick

woo-oo-woo

awk-up

o-ot

ke-aw

ky

korr

rrack

ggaagga-ggaagga

spor-spree-spruck-spor-per-rick-rur-ruck

roc

but what if
the invisible is
simply
     the unseen   solid
        black
     tar sticking to your shoe
     ropey old sweater washed up
     along the shoulder
        black
          feather   that solid
            for you to carry home
            with you
            unharmed?

                      [on a feather]

Nesting Ravens

Yes nesting but you didn't come here
     for a sign
          in the slate there's a deeper
              question you can call
                  into it's a slow exchange
                    snow   melt
                        I don't think the quarry's a woman
                            but the way this wall bleeds
                                  while you wait you can try to eat

a flake or two
     the task is mineral
          wasn't that what you had in mind
             when slate breathes you notice
                the chill it's a hundred years
                  since the quarry's been
                    worked   so
                      time to plan
                          well you can unearth
                            a pillow it'll weigh

you   down   feathers
     couldn't lift a wing
          if they weren't hollow
             listen
                old element I may be
                  making this up--

                                        [on an egg]

2

Since Mars won't be this close to Earth again

in 60,000 years

                    it comes

                    to light

through a haze of stars

    so far off   space
                turns
to time   when
        to where

                    among
                light   years
            I am
            this
            moment

            of
            perception--

[on a mobile]

17

LOOK INSIDE TO SEE IF YOU'VE WON

That summer, butterflies flew regularly into oncoming traffic. We had become a race of giants and could not stop for them. We drove our inflated cars to our box stores and filled our giant shopping carts. Give us the images, we cried. On the sides of delivery trucks there were giant tomato slices, squares of yellow cheese. FREE SUNDAES W/CHICKEN PROMOTIONS! Someone had to arrange the letters on the sign. We had become a race of giants, every generation outgrowing the last. White admirals hovered at the level of the grilles. They were doing what they've always done, which is to flutter. Our vehicles had the blunt, aggressive faces of tanks. With fists too big for our forks, we cleaned our plates and ordered the dessert with sprinkles. The butterflies were not trying to tell us anything and anyway we wouldn't have noticed. It was such a pretty drive.

[on a box]

Seal   Rock

call the split   between us
marriage   this slab of husband
set against me   for warmth
after twenty odd years   no one I know
better   I should
know   better
flipping sand   on our backs
wallowing   to seal   lips
lying   two   fold
a couple   of stones
stones   in the wall

[on split slate]

swallow

the words
he said
we
don't
want
them
all over
the map
of
your
tongue
and if
they
burn
the roof
of
your
mouth
we don't
want
them
jumping
to

safety

[on a tongue depressor]

Hardwood

Ash

    say ash   a fire laid
                    with three logs
                    because a fire must have

    something   to aspire to

                third log on top   to catch

                this silence

                    the fire needs to burn
                    the fire needs to burn
                                up

    sometimes I'm just split wood
        sometimes I'm what's caught
            a quiet thing

                    trying to say
                      ash
                      again

                      ash

                    [on a log]

3 Sent to Susan Walp on 9/9

                    1   milk
         thin clouds south this evening
         1 -- 2 --   -- 4! monarchs
                    skim over
              the same

              white pine

                                   [in a milkweed pod]

                    2 Schadenfreude

     when the car following too close goes off the road
         when my blind friend walks into a chair
                         there
         is no joy more terrible than this

                                   [on a glass shard]

                    3 coquelicot

              caught in the wind how
              can I bear the brilliance   of things

                    passing--

                                   [on red silk]

11 Sentences

Making vinegar was the only trade open to lepers.

There is a small fee for tying quilts, unless you are over 65, in which case the service is free.

One bird, which needed to have its claw treated for an infection, squirmed while held, screaming "I have a question."

A closely watched measure of risk sentiment is the volatility index.

Your identity is valuable; if someone steals it to commit fraudulent acts, it can affect every aspect of your life.

Floral sources include wildflower.

A good persistence is the sign of an interesting wine.

Private capital, too, can flow to where it is well treated, and can do so as never before.

Group zero comprises the noble gases.

Dogs tremble with cold when menthol is injected into their blood.

Meditation was deprived of her arms to be incorporated into the monument to Victor Hugo, where she embodies poetry.

[on paper strips woven through my liver scan]

Not Even Glass

keeps me

from the other side

where a dying moth
--one life already crawling
--one life already egg

beats its wings

against the pane

and a meteor will stun me
if I can stay awake

and a verb

slows enough to hold that
glass

is really
fluid
and ripples

over   time--

[on an old window]

crossroad

like
lichen
we
now
live
on
nothing
at
all

[on a change-of-address form]

Gris-gris is a powerful charm.

gris-gris   this is written on the night sky
    this is written in the rain

           In geologic time, the days were getting
           longer, .002 sec./century. As Earth ground
           to a halt, humankind was a violent
           force that destroyed the living
           face of the planet.

gris-gris   this is written in ashes
    this is written in stone

           The elections were over. In one house
           a family was watching a movie about
           an orphan and a garden. Baghdad, the mother
           was thinking, raging, such fire
           in her own savage heart.

gris-gris   this is written in November
    this is written in blood

           How had it grown so dark.
           The daughter smiling now because
           the roses were
           blossoming, the orphan and
           the animals were making friends.

           [in stone]

One of Magic's Most Beautiful Illusions

the escape artist announces as the stage lights are lowered
he folds his wife into an impossibly small box then sticks
swords through it he saws the top half from the bottom spins
her head one way her legs another we can still see her face she's
smiling now he opens the box he offers her his hand smiling
she steps out but
she isn't
smiling is she when he chains his own wrists and ankles
and climbs into the vat full of water and locks it from the
inside no she's counting the seconds she's checking
her watch she's holding her
breath because this is serious you
can tell he's doing something
very brave and he is really
in danger

[on bravery]

1-800-FEAR

We'd like to talk with you about fear they said so
many people live in fear these days they drove up
all four of them in a small car nice boy they said
beautiful dogs they said so friendly the man ahead
of the woman the other two waiting in the drive I
was outside digging up the garden no one home I said
what are you selling anyway I'm not interested I
said well you have a nice day they said here's our
card there's a phone number you can call anytime
any other houses down this road anyone else live
here we'd like to talk to them about living in fear

[on fear]

Stitch

in the children's hospital
emergency room
christmas eve

— — —

for there's been some posturing
on either side

— — —

tracks between snow banks

— — —

an episiotomy is easier
to suture   still most women
and midwives prefer tears

— — —

         the pin scars
   rust where

— — —

around my wrist
    to save
  my marriage

- - -

please (in)   I'm sorry (out)

- - -

what
      I've dropped
      been left in (plural)
      haven't had to wear
      wasn't wearing
      here look
      my broken needles

- - -

        oh go on

                    [on 9 sheets of vellum, hand sewn]

30

3

glyph

      what | made
    of the body
      incised

           that writing began
          in this
            posture

                  bent over —
                faces
                  the ground

                                    [on a salt flat]

Great Salt Lake

1
North Shore

--Spiral Jetty

that Robert Smithson left
                his question
mark   hanging
          out   there   in   the   question
                              that needs to be asked

                    so huge
                how an entire
          city   can ignore it
                take the name
                          Salt Lake

          so   often   now   I'm   searching
      for   a   word   and   I   can't   find   it
have to skirt
                    around
                                              say it another

          way

look at any word long enough
*   and you will see it open*
into a series

             of faults, a terrain
         of particles, each
                 containing its own void
                                        Smithson wrote
          but also   *the names of minerals*
     and the minerals themselves do not differ
         from each other   salt
       cuts the feet   it hurts
                   to look into the   lake

          water   glistening   dead
pelicans   float   up   near   the   oil   seep   where   I
          return   a   skull   to   a   pair
     of   wing   bones   empty   cartridges
     everywhere   the   shoreline's   mostly   used
         for   a   shooting
              range
I   collect   them   making   a   nest   on
              driftwood

     a series of faults
                      these shells   *each containing*
          its own void
                      still what I want to say
          with them   the words
               hatch   don't they   all beak
and broken feather
                              the crystals
                    grow--

2
South Shore

placenta means
      flat cake   *a fluke*
                  this old
sea   floor   salt
            flat
               of course
      after   birth
it can't support
              what life I am
    now
         but what life
was
           I

              from the access road
                  wet ooze
                  my footprints

                  the beached grebes

                        wading ankle
              deep
                  into brine
           shrimp

                        rounding back
             into egg

```
     from the highway who'd guess
we were
          viable              a life
line  of  matted  feathers  rank
          behind barbed
wire                         who'd check


                          yet I am

                        re
                        membered



                   when the lake takes me       in


                          what puts on
                                  my shoes
                        what blows toward
                                      the road   leaving
                          against the fence
                                      that ragged
                              sack
```

Milk

     baby pronghorn carcass   splayed
toward Antelope   Island   neck twisted
                          twisted
                              like a loose tooth
                         like a rag wrung into a teat
                                 for the orphaned

     young   the mother   licked   just once
before she turned to nurse   her own grief
     rising thick   as that longing   that is both thirst and hunger

     before they separate and are given names

In Land

> the questions as to whether the land was of a mineral or agricultural
>   character
> so, too, is the key to my hut

1   *our subject is the bitter fragment*

however his name attaches to the great fossil body
neither am I a wild beast
black, as it really is, with a thin scumbling of
atmospheric cobalt
myself in unbroken ostracism

2   *books and a raven*

this one of endless effrontery and sidelong gait
yet this wild was not sought by me that I might escape the sex
for the raven I have made a door of his own
on the other hand is my easel
even among the democratic rocks
I turn to my books

3   *it is in its way a perfect thing*

redeeming the waste
the sifters are prompt

it is easier to gather than to create
in the wildest meaning, this guano-dust is scattered

4   *not through pride, shall I be brought to the eating of grass*

skirt my island as often as I will
carrion of some kind has drifted ashore
being wingless, I cannot pass

5

a half-circle beach of oolitic sand
clouds of predictive bloom
some pungent and nameless flower
I would have thought that time was truth itself

6

a piece of rude and sterile
rude and unarranged mass
on a limited scale, it has beetling cliffs

7   *not yet the Monk's-hood had bloomed*

and the transplanted fish
have lived and thriven
soon is superceded the native denizen

pioneers were the trout
in that aforetime tenantless lake

8   *not of roses do the sifters dream*

my eyes ache

in the fierce disquiet of time
                              outnoise

beauty may become so perfect that there is
left no room for peace

                   today the same as yesterday

9   *oozing alkali*

malevolent and envenomed
that squat, stealthy motion of theirs

10

evil is not merely negation
no, evil is not merely negation
with the elemental around me, here, if anywhere,
I may test the thought

11   *that mound of oolitic sand, which stands a mystery*

and grief? here it has been
here the old bones, the fossils, the remains of
an hour I lay on the cliff-top
air and water, too, are filled with the ministers of pain
as for the sifters, they have made some charcoal
the sky seems water, the water sky

not without weariness are clouds
these reactionary storms
perhaps, after all, my belief was at fault
tonight we illumined the island with a driftwood fire
when the great conoidal hill lay pale

Art is an Act

                      not self

of   **violence**

           against   will not be gainsaid
                         will brook no argument
                         won't suffer the fools

                                            gladly

          would I climb a
      mountain   of   salt   with   you

before dawn   lodestar   my freight   **the violent**

      silence   the most beautiful   word

                        is

                  trespass

(lucidity is the wound

closest to the sun
       sorry if you've said and I've forgotten
            but
                 were you (the one)
                              raped
                                   by your father

      a cousin
    at a family   re
                      union   a rape
              baby
                      I'm sorry
I
      should
              remember

      have
        we already
                      ad
                      dressed

                      the wound

how do you (ad)dress the wound?)

46

hill wife

beside the grave
the ties gave

was she there
everywhere

in the fern
or return

when he called her
of black alder

on her lips
the fresh chips

or felled tree
she was free

and no child
and too wild

two witches

crone

I'm still here
still smoke and I still
drink but oh I miss them
you know John
he shot himself and Mary
breast cancer and she
had had a child
you know a girl well
she tracked us down
has children of her own
now we wouldn't have
done that we'd have
let her stay home and
keep the baby oh he
was sick I think I
mean he had something
he wasn't well he
came to say goodbye

the night before Young
John he comes to see
me with his boyfriend
wants to know if they
invite me to their
wedding will I come
oh he's a handsome
boy well he always was

girl

you're not afraid are you
big girl like you I was watching
their horse mouth hay he and my
father stall in the shadows I wasn't
listening except to the horse's jaw
except when he said that because
earlier the way he reached for me
yes I was afraid

old man

                         I felt

up my daughter on vacations I
    tried to finger her underwater
       well I was entitled

                   to the oil the water

glass tucked under one arm
    spilled when I bent to pick up mail
       I'd forgotten

               it was full sometimes

I dreamed about disasters I don't believe I
    caused the explosions off shore ash the mountain
       running red

             Sundays the lamb

I carved fed the sons I fathered to protect
    my holdings my wife means to
       stand by

          me to the last

witness tree

     because a forest is *storied*

when it's brought down

the evidence piles up
     even small tracts like this one--the understory

sticks in your throat
the violated the broken
and who's to tell
     if the witness

     tree gets cut
off--stump among all their limbs
in heaps

like shelters

only how could these house
the living--no **way**

in or out no **way**
through--except for smoke--irrevocable

     the mangled cords--

                    on fire

woodpile

1)   dogs of war

            how they keep us chained

                              to terrify the prisoners

                                          that they unchained us

                how the overstory was twisted

                              by storm winds

                                    that they could uproot us

                              if we strained
              to break free   to hold our ground

                how they didn't

                                          that we just snapped
                how our teeth gleam like salt

                                    that we bay

2)   woman warrior

      downed
      girl
      breast
      removed
      for bearing
      arms child
      I never
      was
      allowed
      to play
      with

3) felled

veteran
boy
at
heart
dead
so
long
we shouldn't
feel this but the deaf old man
        is starting up his chain saw--

you who loved me
to stretch my full length
what
warmth
can
I offer
you
now

broken
match
smouldering

birches

its top
    could bear no more

        willfully misunderstand
            then come back and begin over
                    (one eye is weeping)

        too much
                    I'm weary and so I dream
                through air
                        to ground

too soon

                        he learned
                to conquer
                over and over again
                        he found himself the storm

                before them   girls
                        their trunks seem not to break

                    dragged to the withered bracken
                shattering the sun's   turn   click   loaded

                    you must have seen them
                            across
                                    the lines

hill wife

weeping
weeping
for the lost
yet they
are
be
held
here
be
cause
cleaved
I
opens
in the light
the
matrix
gendered

4

Bark Beetle Fragments in Regional Dialects

1   Southwestern

through think on thin   commercial
          success going under
                strip malls
                                              they've ruined
                                     m●y quiet   cul-de-sac

         whole up

Engraven cavern splinters
        surfacing for   float
    for crack   salt in
            tripartite
        ●'ve gnawed back and fir
    on this   yo● dug it
            pointed spineless to the other

Side   pockets densely   but it's not
    a disease   ached tall in the wind by yo●
            O   best   loved
    most vertical among   rock gulls
                        beset
                        aside

        awashed in ●s

3   Red Turpentine Beetle (Northeastern)

                              lightivore

                                             would have cut stars

               but of

                                    more than ●

          could chew

               a fibrous skyful

                                        black holes
                                        all no through

but yes!   horizon   up against   basal
               lines cleanly spit
        way clear   !
               this is o●r boredom of heaven

After the Vote to Mass Discontinue Unmapped Invisible Town Roads

how will we find
   each other?   being
   of the same tribe

                        these letters   picked
                   from our letters

                              bagged

                              for tea

                              steep for three minutes:
                                 this road
                        cut   from
                                 your place to mine

                                 [in a tea bag]

65

Habitat

why
I
am
like
this
place
is
beautiful
and
cold

.

[on an icicle]

The Origins of Bark Beetle as a Written Language

They came down out of the hills, stepping over the cracks where the light
broke through the wood.

        Wood said one and they remembered how to name the matrix
                                 was also to address it.

They practiced walking off their anger.
They dug holes to mark how far they walked.
Then they could come back to the farthest point.
They could compare the lengths of their angers and which was greatest.

When the first line divided earth from sky that was when they began to count.
They counted 1: horizon
                but soon they got bored
                because 2 was only two lines
          whereas 1 had marked what was
                                 from
          what   was

                              not.
1)   they grew confident in their sharp nibs;
2)   they grew tall and beautiful in the way of shadows;
3)   would have been glyphs

                         they never sign with a flourish
Henceforth nothing would prevent them from achieving their signatures.
                    first yo• must learn to write yo•r name

Translator's note: this translation takes some liberties with the original, which
appears to be a very early form of Bark Beetle.

Lawn Furniture

looks out to stars
      so far away
they've long stopped burning

                    Unfathomable Mystery!
      chair I always sit in

      no emptier than the chair
              I never do

ILLUSTRATIONS

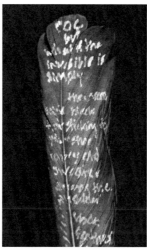

page 11
roc
paint on feather
1½ x 7½ inches

page 17
Since Mars won't be...
ink on wire and paper mobile
4 x 20 inches

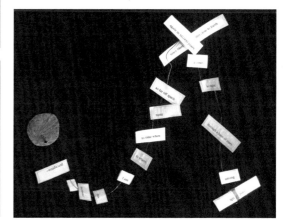

page 12
Nesting Ravens
ink on egg
1½ x 2½ inches

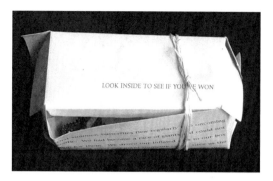

page 18
LOOK INSIDE...
ink on box tied with raffia
2 x 2½ x 5 inches

page 20
swallow
ink on tongue depressor
¾ x 6 inches

page 19
Seal Rock
paint on split slate
1½ x 6 x 17 inches

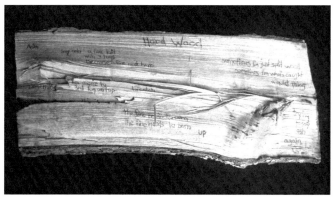

page 21
Hardwood
burned into split log
3 x 7 x 15½ inches

page 23
11 Sentences
ink on paper and liver scan
9 x 14 inches

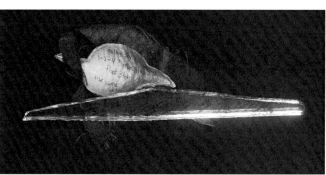

page 22
3 Sent to Susan Walp...
ink on milkweed pod; glass shard; red silk
1 x 3; 1 x 8½; 1 x 6 inches

page 24
Not Even Glass
paint on window pane
7 x 9 inches

page 25
crossroad
ink on mail
change-of-address form
5½ x 7¼ inches

page 26
Gris-gris is a...
paint on split slate
3¼ x 5½ x 7 inches

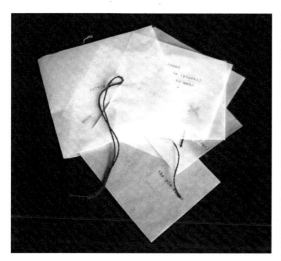

page 66
Habitat
incised on icicle, melted
2 x 8 inches

page 29
stitch
ink, embroidery thread on
    vellum, 9 sheets
3 x 3½ inches

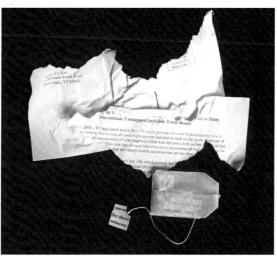

page 65
After the vote...
ink on paper, tea bag
1¾ x 2 ¾ inches

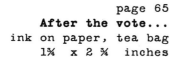

pages 47-56
hill wife
selected photographs

witness tree

hill wife

woman warrior

78

NOTES

The original Bark Beetle texts appear
with the translations as graphite
rubbings.

"Roc" is for Gustaf Sobin.

9/9 was a holiday in ancient China,
the ninth day of the ninth lunar month,
celebrated by climbing a mountain,
contemplating mortality and drinking
chrysanthemum wine.

Gris-gris translates from French as
"gray-gray," the first and most basic
meaning of this incantation.

The poems in section 2 are transcribed
from the objects or materials noted. See
Illustrations.

The poems in section 3 began as collab-
orations with specific sites and other
poets. The Salt Lake poems were made

with Holly Simonsen at the Great Salt
Lake. "In Land" is extracted from *Our
Inland Sea: The Story of a Homestead*,
Alfred Lambourne's record of his attempt
to settle Gunnison Island in the Great
Salt Lake, originally published by The
Deseret News, Salt Lake City, Utah,
1909. The Hill Wife poems were made
with Suzanne Heyd at the Frost Place,
Franconia, New Hampshire. They began as
an installation in a wooded area dis-
rupted by severe storms and subsequent
logging, from which emerged these fig-
ures. The first "hill wife" and "birches"
are lifted from Frost poems, upended.
"Birches" is for Jean Valentine.

"Art is an act of violence against the
violent silence." --Ralph Angel

"Lucidity is the wound closest to the
sun." --René Char

ACKNOWLEDGMENTS

Grateful acknowledgment is made to the following journals where these poems have appeared:

AGNI: "girl"
CAFÉ REVIEW: "Gris-gris is a powerful charm," "Hardwood," "Nesting Ravens"
ECOPOETICS: "Spending Most of Their Time in Galleries...," "Engraver Beetle Cycle." Reprinted in *The Arcadia Project* (Ahsahta Press).
JUBILAT: "Lawn Furniture"
MOUNTAIN INTERVAL: "hill wife"
POETRY MISCELLANY: "1-800-FEAR"
TERRAIN.ORG: "Seal Rock," "swallow," "crossroad"
WILDERNESS MAGAZINE: "LOOK INSIDE TO SEE..."

Deepest thanks to all my collaborators.

Jody Gladding's most recent poetry collection is *Rooms and Their Airs*. Her translations include Jean Giono's *Serpent of Stars* and Pierre Michon's *Small Lives*, which won the Florence Gould and French-American Foundation Translation Prize. She has been a Yale Younger Poet, Stegner Fellow at Stanford, Poet-in-Residence at The Frost Place, and has received a Whiting Writers' Award and Centre National du Livre de France Translation Grants. Her work also includes collaborative site-specific installations that explore the interface of language and ecology. She teaches at Vermont College of Fine Arts and lives in East Calais, Vermont.

Interior design and typesetting by Jeenee Lee.
The font used in this book is Secret Service Typewriter.